Mark T. Craven

A Life Lived Backwards

Reviews of
A Life Lived Backwards

Mark Creaven's new collection of poems, A Life Lived Backwards, *is a starkly lyrical memorial of the harshness of life in the last, rural frontier of Vermont known as the Northeast Kingdom. As an emergency medical technician, a friend, a neighbor, and a caring human being, Mr. Creaven has seen it all: suicide, unspeakable highway wrecks, family violence, livelihoods going up in flames along with house and barns. Yet, in the end,* A Life Lived Backwards *is a tribute to our ability, through love, not just to endure, but to transcend, just about the worst horrors imaginable.*

— Howard Frank Mosher, Vermont author

Shelley wrote in 1821, "In a time of violence, the task of poetry is in some way to reconcile us to our world and to allow us a measure of tenderness and grace with which to exist." Creaven's work A Life Lived Backwards *offers the reader such grace, creating something from the proverbial nothing of life's lacunae in compassion juxtaposed with indifference. Nearly two hundred years after Shelley's* A Defence of Poetry, *Creaven's words hold lyrical ground, offering fragile fortitude and tender, tenuous redemption.*

— Neila Descelles, clinical psychologist

Reviews of
A Life Lived Backwards

Through a full and honorable life that has included service in the military, mental health and emergency medical services Mark Creaven has seen more than his share of the suffering, death and loss that most people carefully protect themselves from experiencing. In the first chapter of A Life Lived Backwards *he gives the reader a rare glimpse into the occasional joy and frequent trauma experienced by emergency workers.*

As an EMS and ER veteran I have become perhaps too numb to traumatic scenes but the jarring imagery of Creaven's poems ripped off my protective layers and lay bare my own unhealed wounds. The concise, evocative and emotionally difficult poems serve their purpose to reader and perhaps writer. Someone must treat the dead and dying and these heroes bear a heavy burden for society. The subsequent chapters contain some lighter passages but continue the theme of devastating loss, still painful to read and effectively exposing my own fears and losses.

There is no refuge here from the reality that people and things die, suffering happens, buildings rot and burn, relationships fail and we all die alone in some sense. Whether redemption is found is up to the reader, but Mark Creaven's important work gives voice to the traumas that fill sleepless nights of millions.

— Paul Newton, M.D., M.M.M., F.A.A.F.P.

A LIFE LIVED BACKWARDS

Poems by an Emergency Medical Technician

Mark T. Creaven, A.E.M.T

Cover image: "Mark" by Ann Young

(Annyoungart.com)

Cover design: Elizabeth S. Trail

ISBN-13:978-1543050264

ISBN-10:1543050263

Dedication

This book is dedicated to my granddaughters, Fiona and Amelia, who allowed me to touch generations to come.

This collection would not be possible without the hard work of Elizabeth Trail who demanded my best; to Francis Lynch, my high school English teacher who taught me about music and poetry; and to Ann Young, the artist who made me look better than I am.

CONTENTS

 # INTRODUCTION

These poems are written for all that serve, have served or will serve their neighbors, their friends and strangers.

In small town emergency medicine it is common for our crews to see friends in distress. Often they see you and say "I'm so glad it's you."

The burden is doubled. After the call, regardless of the outcome, we will see these people again in the market, playing cards, at weddings, in the day-to-day living in small towns. We cannot escape having seen their tears, their fears, their horrors on the worst day of their lives.

Although these poems are divided into three parts, they are in reality woven together. When you are not in an ambulance you still have your life to live. Loves and losses, deaths and births.

It is hard to find nature soothing when you are lying in the snow, in the dark, feeling a neighbor's blood seeping through the bandages and warming your hands.

In addition, families of providers get used to missed meals and missed holidays. They bear the additional burden of the silences as various horrors filter through the mind of their loved ones.

— *Mark Creaven*

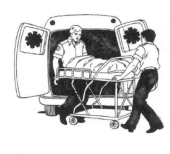

IN THE FIELD

Only

It was only when the wreckers

pulled the car from the water

and the bodies recovered

I could relax.

In the blue early morning cold

some other family grieved.

Not my family. Not today.

It was only when I saw

the tangled mash of a Harley

I could relax,

knowing the crumpled body

with the broken "S"

in the ditch was

not my family. Not today.

Not yet.

⌘

Christmas Eve

I've spent nights waiting,
staring at the walls in the dark,
unable to sleep…

Waiting for the tones.
Puked on. Bled on. Cried on.

Walking into people's lives,
picking them up from their floors.

For a while they become me
and I become them.

I go home alone.
Who will save me?

⌘

She Chooses

She had starved herself
For three days and nights.

Wanting to join her husband
Who had gone on before.

Nothing about life could we offer
To keep her from her path.

Not love. Not beauty. Not kindness.
We watched her go.

⌘

Bridge

Watching the red taillights
slowly disappear into the
icy black river.
There is no why.

⌘

Face Off

Watching what's left of the kid's face.

Giving oxygen with all the landmarks gone.

Just a guess at where this mother's son breathed

Breathed and breathed

And breathed no more.

⌘

The Crash

When we arrived at the scene
The son was holding his father's hands.
The way a good son would.

Above the hands, both arms
Showing shattered bones and flesh.
"Come back, Dad. Come back.
I'm here with you."

We move in quickly, doing
What we know to do.
Airway. "He's clamped down."
Stop the bleeding. Stabilize C-spine.

There's the chopper. The dead don't bleed.
Now he's in the air,
Damn it's cold out. What's for lunch?

⌘

She'll Dance At Her Prom

It's a warm spring morning
When the tones go off.
The dispatcher's voice,
Different than routine.
In her voice you hear the fear.

On scene the father offers his baby in supplication.
"It's my daughter. She's
Not breathing."
I hold this little life in
my hands.

Bag inflated, pushing air

in gentle puffs.

Watch her chest rise and fall.

Monitor beeps along, slowly

Reading threads of life.

It was a warm spring morning.

She won't remember the day

An old guy saved her life.

But 'til I die,

I will.

⌘

Early Morning Stroke

Bedclothes wrapped about her,

she lay like a swooning woman in the silent pictures,

one hand flung across her forehead, eyes closed.

I look at the young firefighter across the room.

He rocks back and forth quietly.

"Fuck." I say. He smiles a small smile and nods.

This is how a life is done.

Two men she never knew standing in her bedroom,

looking at the woman who died.

⌘

Late Night EMS Thoughts

Late night we sat wondering

the best way of dying.

Suicide is the way to go

we all agree.

No one wants it to be messy

for the crew that comes

to pick up the pieces.

Nods of appreciation for this guy or that

who wrapped himself up before

eating his gun.

A chrysalis of death,

neat and tidy with no rough edges.

Or the lady who killed her cat before

herself. Thoughtful to the end

⌘

Night Terror

She took a long time to die,

her feces formed a trail

from bed to toilet, back to bed.

Oozing, gushing red, brown and tarry black.

It must have been a long, long night

growing weaker by the hour.

Too embarrassed to call for help.

When she did decide

In the end, too late.

⌘

Busy Work

I wish I had done more instead of just holding her hand and breathing for her.

I was too busy doing the things I thought would keep her alive.

I was taking her pulse as she died. I should have bid her goodbye.

I was too busy.

⌘

Washing the Longboard

Cold spray of water arcing

Silver sparks

In the cool night air.

Our breaths seen in puffs

As the blood, almost reluctantly,

Slowly sloshes down the drain.

⌘

Island Dream

The world can't make me cry any more.

I will not give voice to the grief I hold within.

I remember the two men bobbing in the black water with white chunks of ice.

Star-shaped, face down.

I remember the grainy black and white films Mr. O'Hearn showed us in the fifth grade.

Dead marines in the water off Tarawa. They floated star-shaped, gently moving with the waves.

My mind spins back and forth, boy and man. I float star-shaped in the world.

Back and forth.

My circuits of sadness are all burned out.

⌘

Renewal

Old and stale

Too many dead or hurt.

I learned the words to say

To soothe too many strangers' pain.

My granddaughter's hand

Warm and trusting in mine

Brings me back.

⌘

LOVE AND LOSS

Morning

The hole you left in me
On the evening of your going
remains.
I touch the spot where you had lived,
and watch
as the ghosts begin to dance.
I'd like to say that mornings are good,
that at day's first light I do not reach
out to feel your warmth
and know the world is safe for me for
just another day.
But no. Each day starts with a shiver.
Then the wave of sadness sweeps
over me.
Empty bed. Empty life.

⌘

Once

Once you,

once me,

Now us…more…then less…

Then more again.

A place, a way, a path.

Together.

Now a touch. Now a tear.

Touch again.

So little…so much.

⌘

An Accidental Meeting

If it weren't for your scent
I think I could make it.
but close to you I'm like a kid at
the Saturday matinee watching
coming attractions
that I've seen many times before.

⌘

A Year's Passing

Spring days of flowers,

The early warmth of the sun

Summer smells of hay and wild berries

The cool splash of water from the meadow brook.

Fall, especially the nights,

Grey wood smoke and apple cider.

Winter, essence of musk and warmth

Beneath the mounds of down comforters.

When you turn to me, I must

press my cheek against you as I inhale your soul.

⌘

A Habit But Not Love

In the middle of a fitful sleep
I hear you whimper, cry out. Then
murmuring, you reach your arm out
to me.
I feel myself drawn nearer to you
though a gulf of miles sprawls
between us.

⌘

Changes

What shall I tell you?
That since you entered my life,
even before our joining,
I am changed.
With different joy
and different peace
and even different pain.

⌘

Sex

I found the place where we made love last summer.

A grasshopper leapt, its tiny feet clinging to the damp between your breasts.

You laughed and gently brushed it aside, then welcomed me within your body.

Today I tilled the ground to plant the seeds for this winter's food.

The grass in the pasture still bore the imprint of our blanket.

We had left it there last fall with the hope of someday returning.

We never went back, and soon after, you left.

Seed for seed, both spilled on the ground.

Mine now, carefully sown for winter food, staying and growing in life. My other seed, leaking slowly, slowly, from out your loins.

My lord, I wish you were with me.

⌘

Water Woman

I watched you once secretly,

you still wet from a late afternoon swim.

We had hayed all day, and as I stacked the last bales

you slipped away, shucking clothes and laughing as

you startled the ducks and splashed into the pond.

From the high-drive I watched you stand on the

shore, your long brown hair flung into the wind.

I watched you, a woman, and I felt like a little boy

pressing my eye up to the knothole of

the girl's changing room.

Then you turned to me, and flung your arms to me

in open, welcoming embrace

and I, boy in a man's body,

was yours

as long as you would have me.

⌘

First Love

We were both so young
with no idea how crushing life would be.

Together we would sneak off into the maple woods
kisses smooth and new.

Once I slid my hand under her bra and out came
the first and most beautiful breast
I had ever seen.

My lips closed around her nipple
and together we found for the first time
the joy of giving and taking pleasure.

Later her father hung himself
from the tree we used to lean against
and talk about our future.

Too much to deal with,
we lost ourselves in each other's silences
drifting apart wordlessly
connected only in memory.

⌘

A Conversation

In the rich blue tinged light of dawn
He caught just the shadow,
A glimpse of who he had become.

Her words, cool and sad,
"I was happy then. I don't think
I will ever be again."
Something broken. Something torn.

"People change," he said.
And sighed.

⌘

Home

In the warmth of summer sun

We walk, hold hands, touch.

A thought shared. A laugh. Silence.

We see together the struggles each has made

To come to where we are now.

Turning back, we hear the gentle cry.

The little one is calling.

A snuggle. A giggle. A grin.

We are home.

⌘

On Leaving

Holding the little one in my arms last night

his body warm and soft in sleep,

it seemed that the sky would tear

from the pain that sliced through my heart.

I set him back in his wooden bed,

The one I had hewn and carved in celebration of his
birth.

I folded the covers around him,

the little puffing of his breath

the only sound but for the sob

that hung in my throat.

⌘

Night Texting

I winnow through her words
As if the tiny electric scrawl
Would give up its deeper meaning
When seen with my own needy eye.
But they are devoid of any of her intent.
Shifting around with only my own electrons
To show in the magic lantern of my mind
What I wished she had texted.

⌘

Knowing We Will Fight

Waiting for the storm,

I crouch defenseless,

Wondering if the smart retorts I have gathered

Will protect me from the

Pummeling of your anger.

⌘

The Shell Game

They say cicadas wait 17 years in the dark. Then they live and mate and die.

As a child one summer I found their hollow cases. Empty, showing the form of life when life had fled.

I was too busy to mark the next time they appeared, caught up with new wife, and learning how to kill whoever was the latest enemy.

Two births, and two births more, and some new lovers. And the cicadas came and went, marking time within my life.

Now I wait.

I have the time at last to wonder

as my own shell dries,

why the cicadas mark the years easier than I.

⌘

Tired Rage

A woman in the dark

her life ebbing in a black mist

for a stranger's obscene pleasure.

There is no why.

A crazy loser

erasing lives in the dark

the only success he has ever known

is denying others joy.

The bonds that hold us,

the flickering flames

of hope and love.

Are they strong enough?

The world makes no more sense

than we think it does.

We cling to each other

seeking meaning in the dust of days.

⌘

Reflection

Where did the gold-flecked days of summer go?

"Come on Billy, we'll shag flies.
Then we'll go to the salt marsh and see the dead crabs
hung on tall marsh grasses."

"Hey, there's a hornets' nest to poke."

Now run, canvas PF Flyers pounding down the
road...

I look back in terror at the imaginary swarm following
me.

"There's the girls."

They scream and run, but not quite as fast as us.

Barbara's got boobies.

Her blouse with pandas for pockets covering her
buds...

She moves...

Oh my god.

And when the sun shines just behind her...

if we look real hard...

but she catches us looking and....

So off we go

The girls stay in pretended unawareness

and talk that special way that girls seem to do.

Not little girls but not women yet…

I throw a balsa wood glider, its little red plastic pilot
stuck forever, hands gripping the little plastic machine
gun.

I can't pretend the fun is there anymore.

The big kids came years later
and from the sky
They streamed real fire.

Now the ones who fall down don't bounce back up
to change the sides and make them fair.

But then we were John Wayne, GI Joe, Sitting Bull
and Custer righting every wrong.

Oh Lord,
the day is fading.

The street lights blink on.

See you tomorrow. Yes. See you tomorrow.

⌘

What the Son Teaches

It's the son that
Teaches the father
If only the father will hear.

The father looks upon the son
Sees the beauty of the man emerging
And takes pride in what he sees.

But can the gardener take credit
For the rampant colors of
Flowers in the field?

He exists just to bear witness to
The strength of that life that seeks its own truth
The son grows in his own way.

⌘

Legacy

In the leftovers of others' lives, I sit

reading the poems of Garcia-Lorca.

The day hangs over the water, brooding,

slowly chilling the life from my world.

Another chunk of wood to the fire, for

I must drive away the cold that wraps

its tendrils around me.

I need a phoenix, a magic salamander

to rise from the fire and ashes.

I search along the book shelves for another book of
verse, and, finding none,

write these lines.

⌘

VERMONT

Crow

A sharp-inked wave of line
across the icy sky

Grey shadow courses
over crusted snow.

A liquid rasp of sound

Then gone.

⌘

On Killing Pigs

It could have been the pulley
Worn smooth from all the years
Of hoisting pigs in death.

Or the way the rope, ill-stored
From the year before, frayed
And caught the rail.

But whatever the cause,
In the crying rain we stood
Watching a dead, bleeding pig

Swing like some obscene clock part.
Stuck.

⌘

West Glover Farm

The farmhouse clutched the wind-blown land.
It watched as boy came from chores, watched as he
went off to war. Watched as his blood seeped into
some French farmer's field.

(The notice of his being "lost somewhere in France"
yellows in the attic of the house.) Only the house
remembers his feet skip stepping up the foot-worn
stairs.

Later on the barn burned down. No more chores to
do. The cellar hole an empty socket now with flame-
scarred stone crumbling.

The night it lit up, the neighbors came and could do
no more than watch in silent groups as hand-hewn
ribs fell with a sigh,
one upon the other.

It seems like those within this house must meet some
measure imposed.

Drunk one night, again, leaving lights and laughter,
sweat-stained shirts and groping feels, through the
wet, white flakes to home. Alone he lost it on the
curve just past the schoolhouse. Another lesson
learned.

One wheel hung up in the ditch. "Son of a bitch!"

The warm bed seems far, far away
And the mute flakes fall.

By Jesus tho'. Been stuck before.
 Just rock it back and forth.
Should have had another beer
To keep the chill away.

Gloves wet through from frantic digging,
And still the mute flakes fall.
Found in the morning, the neighbors kindly
Closed the bulging, frost-rimmed eyes,
breaking shards of frozen tears.

Three months later when the ground grew
Soft enough to till, the neighbors stuck him
(and several others neatly stored away 'til thaw)
In the earth.

A few words, but it's hard to carry
Sorrow three months, harder still to mourn
When the smell of life is on the winds of spring

One winter we have limped through.
Three of us now
And the aging house looks on.
We count ourselves alive but hurt
Bruised by too-long nights beside the hissing firebox.

Wondering now the price the house or fate or god
Will charge for seeing summer in.

⌘

Young's Barn Burned

On the day the barn caught fire
no one could have known that God, the jester,
would take the bales of summer hay,
would take the sweat and strain of calloused hands
and destroy what they had built.

The still-green bales sat in humid darkness,
kept warm by their own silent secret.
Each day the sun would filter through
the tired old boards that kept just most
of the rain and wind and snow outside.

A dozen new-hatched swallows each year
would use the old hewn beams'
elbows and shoulders to test their wings.
then they would soar on puffs of summer air

While down below the men and boys
and women and girls
would sweat and curse and laugh and moan
putting the winter's hay away.

The men fought to free the silken cows
and drive them to the autumn air.
But the cows sought out the safety of the place
the only place they knew to go,
the stalls where they had spent
the long, cold winter
thinking what it is to be a cow.

 In their stalls where they stood, quivering,
when the floor above gave way
to cascade bales of burning hay,
in the place they knew and maybe loved
they died.

⌘

Aftermath

Barns always look so small after they've burned,
their beams all gone, the twisted weavings of chain,
and elevators red and rusting in the rain.
Lying over all, the warped sheets of roofing steel
a child's card game after play.

⌘

Wisdom of the Wood

After the storm had swept through the hills
I chose to walk the path
that wound snake-like through the woods
I was stopped halfway on my journey

An old white pine tree had fallen in the night,
tearing limbs from itself and others as its roots
one by one snapped and tore themselves free from
the rocky ground which anchored them

Now the tree lay sprawling on the land,
dying,
no longer rising high above
the moldering leaves of summers past.

And in its fall, its great mass
had rent the sighing winds
and smashed a small green stand of saplings,
sprung over time from its seeds.

"People aren't like trees," I wished,
and walked back home
while the wind made the white pines nod.

On the Beauty of Nature

1.

Chicken, you don't know
the face of death even
with his red fur face
leering at you from
the tall green grass.
Today you will die.

2.

Hawk, blur of taloned death,
screaming dive, feathers
tumble, dipped in blood.
Did I really see?
Suddenly I am chilled

3.

Fox, I watched too

long, too many days,

as you practiced to become

a chicken slayer. I held

you in my sights, but

your beauty stopped my trigger finger

and I wished you well.

⌘

Christmas Present

As a child I waited breathless

for the sound of hooves on the roof,

Santa spewing toys and presents under the tree.

Old now, I see the magic

not in myths

but in the smiles, the hopes of years and years

piling one atop the other.

⌘

Screw it

I don't like to read

the words that other poets write.

For if they write of life

Or love, or death,

and they do it in a way

I do not yet understand,

I grumble "I could write it better."

And if in reading their work

I feel the shifting in my gut,

the awakening of my eyes

as if my own secret thoughts and feelings

lay exposed upon the page,

I know how feeble are my own scribblings.

I wish I did one thing well

⌘

A Better Deal

When she went away,

He got the empty house.

She got everything else.

And still he counted himself ahead.

⌘

Glare

"Don't the sun just burn your eyes so late on these days in winter?"

"These here tears? They're from the glare and the wind that whirls and sucks around us."

"Why no. I'm not crying. It's the way the light has made me look."

"I'm as fine, as good, as strong as ever. Just slow your pace a bit."

I'm not the man I used to be and maybe never was.

One leg free and one with frozen knee, I crab across the crusted snow.

"It's just the sun and just the wind. Please slow your pace for me. The glare just blinds my eyes.

⌘

Broken

The tiny gold chain
graced round her neck
above the sweat
that gathered glowing on her breasts.

In a thoughtless caress I broke that chain.
It slowly slid past her shoulder
Then a golden tangle on the bed beneath her.
Lost.

⌘

Ending

These poems are alien things,
dredged up from unexplored depths.

They gasp in the light
 Sucking putrid slime.

They try to live without
disclosing too much of me.

⌘

62nd Company Reunion

The warriors gather
Among old friends
Living and dead.

The laughs louder,
The silences deeper.
They read the names
Of those who went before.

No man really lost
While memory lasts.

A bell is rung and echoes
Through the room.
Names read. Names
Choked in their throats.

Shadow flashes of memories
Of this man or that man.

Some who died under fire.
Others slowly dying from
Poisons sprayed to choke the
Green life that hid the enemy.

These same poisons now
Strangling the lives
Of those who thought they
Were only doing good.

Now the pain passes on to the
Families, the wives, the lovers,
Children and children's children.

While the men fall
into the column of warriors
that reaches back in history
The ranks of heroes who died.

Author's Note

The place I live in is called the Northeast Kingdom.

To live in the Kingdom is to learn many survival skills. The life is hard. The winters are long. Cold creeps into your soul.

One winds up having many different jobs. I have been a teacher, a logger, a drug counselor, a photographer, an advertising rep, and an advanced level Emergency Medical Technician (AEMT).

Now retired, I live alone with my cat who has no name.

Artist Ann Young

The cover art is an oil painting of Mark Creaven by Ann Young of Barton, Vermont.

Ms. Young is an oil painter with a passion for color. She started her career in ceramic and wood sculpture before moving into painting. She holds a BFA from the Rhode Island School of Designs and has shown extensively in Vermont and New York City.

Contact her at *annyoung773@gmail.com* or *annyoungart.com*

Elizabeth Trail, Editing and Cover Design

This book is edited by Elizabeth Trail.

Ms. Trail is a reporter at *the Chronicle* in Barton, Vermont. In her spare time she does web design, book layouts, and cover design.

Contact her at *hartwellpond@gmail.com*